Class 67

MARK V. PIKE

KEY Books

BRITAIN'S RAILWAYS SERIES, VOLUME 30

Front cover image: Rounding the long curve away from what used to be called Aller Junction, just west of Newton Abbot, 67016 and 67024 are starting the climb up to Dainton with UK Railtours 'Mazey Day in Penzance' charter. With over 6,000hp available, there would be no problem tackling this stiff climb up to the summit at Dainton Tunnel. 26 June 2010.

Back cover image: On a lovely fresh early summer morning, we see Colas Rail 67027 *Charlotte* on the rear of 1Q23, the 05.41 Reading Triangle Sidings to Salisbury, passing near the village of Motcombe, situated just a couple miles east of Gillingham (Dorset), on the edge of the delightful Blackmore Vale. 28 June 2018.

Title page image: Arriva Blue and ex-Chiltern silver cab to cab in the stabling sidings at Didcot Parkway. 20 May 2015.

Contents page image: In all forms of photography, sometimes you just get really lucky! This is Colas Rail 67023 *Stella* arriving back at Salisbury beneath a perfect rainbow with 1X23, the 15.13 Salisbury to Salisbury (via Southampton Central). It absolutely poured down just minutes prior to the train's arrival, with the sunshine suddenly appearing to form that super rainbow. 27 August 2020.

Published by Key Books
An imprint of Key Publishing Ltd
PO Box 100
Stamford
Lincs PE19 1XQ

www.keypublishing.com

The right of Mark V. Pike to be identified as the author of this book has been asserted in accordance with the Copyright, Designs and Patents Act 1988 Sections 77 and 78.

Copyright © Mark V. Pike, 2022

ISBN 978 1 80282 206 9

Typeset by SJmagic DESIGN SERVICES, India.

Contents

Introduction

During 1998, English, Welsh & Scottish Railway (EWS) decided that it needed to replace its ageing fleet of Class 47/7 locomotives currently being used on passenger, mail and charter trains. For each of these operations, the company concluded that a high-speed, high-powered loco would be required. After a bit of research, EWS contracted Alstom in Spain for an order of 30 Class 67 3,200hp diesel-electric locos, owned by Angel Trains but to be leased by EWS. The first of these locos, 67003, was delivered to Newport Docks in October 1999. Before being delivered to the UK, 67002 was extensively tested on a high-speed rail line in Spain, where it reached a top speed of 143mph.

All subsequent locos were delivered to the UK by ship to Newport Docks. The locos' first revenue-earning duties were in the west of England, on the mail trains that they were built for. Although they were designed to operate at speeds of up to 125mph, it was found that heavy axle loadings might cause damage to the permanent way at these speeds. This caused them to be limited to 110mph, and they have never regularly operated at 125mph on the UK network.

During 2003, after the fleet had only been in service for a few years, Royal Mail announced the end of its partnership with EWS, with the last Travelling Post Offices and bulk mail trains running during early 2004. The company cited the high costs of rail compared to moving parcels and mail by road and air. EWS proclaimed that this would inevitably add thousands of lorries to the UK road system but, unfortunately, this had no influence over Royal Mail's decision.

With the main duty that the class was built for now removed, EWS had to find other jobs for these practically new locomotives. Due to the high axle loading mentioned earlier, the locos were actually quite limited on the routes they could work over, especially some of those in Scotland. Eventually though, the fleet was reassigned to various duties throughout the UK, such as fast freight trains (though not heavy ones) and various charter train duties. The locos also found themselves working spells on timetabled passenger services on various occasions with First Great Western, Wrexham & Shropshire and ScotRail, while they also have a long-standing duty acting as thunderbird rescue locos on the East Coast Main Line.

Currently, in the early 2020s, much of the fleet is not fully utilised and, as a result, quite a few have found themselves in storage, with a couple being used as a source of spares. It remains to be seen if any of these will ever return to service.

Chapter 1

Parcels and Mail Trains

These trains were the main reason the locos were constructed in the first place. They were to replace the fleet of ageing and increasingly unreliable Class 47s that were then in use on these trains. Unfortunately, after just a few years, this traffic ceased.

Only just over two years old and still looking quite new, this is the penultimate loco of the fleet. 67029 is awaiting mail bags to be loaded at Exeter St Davids before heading away with an unidentified northbound parcels train. 15 August 2002.

Just a few months old, this is 67025 standing at the pre-rebuilt Reading station with 1V33, the 15.58 Willesden to Plymouth via Bristol. Circa 2000.

This time it is 67002 hauling 1V33, the 15.58 Willesden to Plymouth, west through Didcot Parkway. This loco was involved in a serious crash at Lawrence Hill (Bristol) on 1 November 2000, when a Royal Mail train passed red signals and ran into the back of a coal train at around 03.30. The mail train was travelling at around 50mph when the incident occurred and, such was the force of the impact, the loco climbed over the top of the coal train, coming to rest about 50 yards later on top of one of the wagons and wedged against the A420 Church Road bridge that crosses the line at Lawrence Hill station. The driver of the mail train suffered a broken arm and various cuts and bruises but, thankfully, there were no other injuries. To date, this is the only serious accident to befall one of the fleet. Circa 2000.

Special Delivery

Passing the site of what became the location of the serious breach of the sea wall in February 2014, 67013 is seen approaching Rockstone Footbridge with 1C91, the 13.53 Plymouth to Bristol Temple Meads. The area of the breach was on the left of the picture, where the people are walking along the low section; in fact, even at this date, the wall did look a tad buckled! During the rebuild, this low section was raised right up to the height of the rest of the wall, thus giving much more protection from the waves. 8 August 2001.

This is 67009 coming round the curve on the approach to Newton Abbot station, once again working 1C91, the 13.53 Plymouth to Bristol Temple Meads, the day before the previous image. 7 August 2001.

This time we see 67026 catching the setting sun as it passes Marine Parade at Dawlish with 1M65, the 19.15 Plymouth to Willesden Royal Mail Terminal (RMT). 15 August 2002.

It was not unusual to see more than one loco on mail trains at the time; sometimes this was due to the failure of the train loco or, far more commonly, just a loco balancing move. This is 67028 and 47776 *Respected* passing through Newport station with an unidentified service bound for Swansea. 22 November 2002.

The same service as seen in the previous picture has gone one better here, with an extra Class 67! 67006, 67028 and 47734 *Crewe Diesel Depot Quality Approved* are also passing through Newport station. The view here has now changed somewhat with the coming of electrification. 1 July 2003.

This time the boot is on the other foot as we see 47749 *Atlantic College,* 67015 and 67025 departing the loop at Dawlish Warren with 5C43, the 09.19 Bristol Barton Hill to Plymouth empties. It is interesting to note that the Class 47 is still in service in 2021 and soon to enter its 56th year in traffic. It is currently working for GBRf and used for hauling various units around the country. It has also been reunited with its original *City of Truro* nameplates. 29 September 2003.

Before the low fence was erected here, spoiling the view somewhat, 67016 is passing the well-known location at Cockwood Harbour, near Starcross, with 1E41, the 17.23 Plymouth to Low Fell (Newcastle) service. 30 September 2003.

Approaching Dawlish station is 67010 *Unicorn* with 1E43, the 15.09 Plymouth to Low Fell. This loco later went on to do a spell north of the border, operating the Caledonian Sleeper trains and wearing a deep blue livery. It is now in DB Cargo bright red, with the nameplates having been removed many years ago. 10 August 2001.

Unicorn

Having just dropped down from the notorious Rattery incline, this is 67015 coasting through Totnes station with 1C91, the 13.53 Plymouth to Bristol Temple Meads service. 30 July 2002.

A relatively recent image, which is now impossible to replicate because of the reconstruction of the sea wall in the early 2020s, 67011 passes over the short viaduct at Dawlish with 5C43, the 09.19 Bristol Barton Hill to Plymouth empties. 15 August 2002.

Not perhaps the standard view that one usually sees of a train at Starcross. This is 67002 *Special Delivery* snaking around the reverse curves with 1E43, the 15.09 Plymouth to Low Fell service. 30 September 2003.

Passing the well-known landmark of the former broad gauge pumping house near Starcross station, 67023 approaches with 1E43, the 15.09 Plymouth to Low Fell. Initially, all of the fleet were limited to a speed restriction of 110mph due to high axle loadings, which lead to modifications to the bogies. 67023 was the first of the class to receive these modifications and was passed for 125mph running in July 2001, although this speed capability has never been actually utilised in the UK beyond some test runs. 15 August 2002.

This is 67011 passing under Coastguard footbridge at Dawlish, once again with 1E43 bound for Tyneside. 6 August 2001.

No need for introductions for this image, as 67002 *Special Delivery* is captured passing through Dawlish with 5C43, the 09.19 Bristol Barton Hill to Plymouth empties. Unfortunately, this view has now been rather compromised with the reconstruction of the sea wall along here. 30 September 2003.

Above: In some nice evening sunshine, 67019 passes the harbour at Cockwood with 1E41, the 17.23 Plymouth to Low Fell service. 15 August 2002.

Left: Curving round towards Dawlish station is 67025 *Western Star* with 1E43, the 15.09 Plymouth to Low Fell. The milepost to the right signifies that this location is 206 and a quarter mile from London Paddington. 29 September 2003.

67009 is seen approaching Sprey Point, between Teignmouth and Dawlish, with 5C43, the 09.19 Bristol Barton Hill to Plymouth empties. 3 October 2003.

Above: This time, 67027 is seen passing Marine Parade at Dawlish with 1C91, the 13.53 Plymouth to Bristol Temple Meads service. 10 August 2001.

Right: 67009 and 67005 *Queen's Messenger* are pictured passing the superb semaphore signal gantry at Lostwithiel with 5M99, the 17.55 St Blazey to Plymouth empties. The use of two locos on this train was almost certainly for loco balancing. 30 August 2002.

67017 *Arrow* and 67011 run through Cardiff Central with 5B03, the 10.34 Bristol Barton Hill to Cardiff Canton Travelling Post Office empties, which was a Fridays-only working at the time. This is another location that has been transformed with the advent of overhead electrification. 8 February 2002.

Chapter 2
Freight Trains

Although the fleet was not designed for hauling heavy freight trains, they have, over the years, been used on some lighter loaded services, often when a more suitable Class 66 was not available. This practice became more regular once the Royal Mail services had ceased.

For a while during the early 2000s, a pair of the class were actually the booked motive power for 6C06, the 11.06 St Blazey to Tavistock Junction china clay empties, once again probably for balancing purposes, but it was certainly quite an unusual sight at the time. 67007 and 67003 are seen winding their way through Plymouth station on this service. 14 March 2002.

This is 67018 *Rapid* coming up the incline towards Beaulieu Road in the New Forest National Park with an Eastleigh Yard to Hamworthy Quay contaminated oil waste (COW) train. These trains ran very sporadically as Q trains (when required) for a few years in the mid-2000s and were quite difficult to photograph as they mostly ran at the drop of a hat, so being in the right place at the right time helped! This was the only occasion a Class 67 worked it as far as I know. The wagons used were OBA four-wheeled wooden-bodied opens that carried removable tank containers for the oil. Upon arrival at Hamworthy Quay, these tanks were unloaded and taken by boat over to Furzey Island, located in Poole Harbour, where the drilling rig is located, for loading, while the wagons themselves remained at Hamworthy. Once loaded, the tanks were tripped back to Hamworthy Quay on the boat and loaded back on the rail wagons. The train was then taken, usually the following day, to the Lowestoft area where it was processed. On this particular day, the loco returned light engine back to Eastleigh, and a Class 66 was sent down from there to collect the train the next day. 26 August 2005.

67002 *Special Delivery* is seen approaching Eastleigh hauling a few flat wagons as 6B44, the 12.04 Southampton Western Docks to Eastleigh Yard trip working. Class 67s were commonly used on this working, often when one or two were in the area for imminent use on charter trains. 3 April 2008.

This is 67004 *Post Haste* passing Millbrook Freightliner terminal with 6B38, the 11.00 MoD Marchwood to Eastleigh Yard. This was another service ideally suited to a Class 67. 24 February 2004.

When it became known that mail trains would cease running in early 2004, other uses were sought for the class, and this entailed more widespread driver training, including at Eastleigh. One of the trains they were often used on was the liquefied petroleum gas (LPG) working that ran at the time to/from Furzebrook on the Dorset coast, near Wareham. While they proved just about acceptable on the empty trains, they were not so good on the loaded ones, especially when it came to the 1 in 60 gradient of Parkstone Bank, near Poole. Quite often, if a Class 67 brought the empties in, it would return back to Eastleigh light engine. These three images depict the southbound empty train. 67029 is seen passing Baiter Park (near Poole) with 6W53, the 08.45 Eastleigh Yard to Furzebrook. Up until the late 1960s, when land reclamation took place, the point at which I am standing would have been quite literally in the mud of Poole Harbour. 8 August 2003.

The use of the class on these trains continued sporadically through 2004 until the service completely ceased in July 2005, with the LPG then going to its destination via a long pipeline. With a wave from the driver, this is 67012 with 6W53, the 08.45 Eastleigh Yard to Furzebrook, on the approach to Poole. 2 June 2004.

This last image of 6W53 shows 67028 doing the honours as it heads through Branksome station heading west on a miserable damp day. 10 September 2004.

Since the repainting of the Royal pair in the mid-2000s, it has always been quite amusing to see them working mundane freight services. This is 67006 *Royal Sovereign* approaching Oxford working 6A49, the 12.10 Didcot Yard to MoD Bicester, and consisting of just two wagons. 8 January 2013.

This time we see 67005 *Queen's Messenger* passing Southampton Central with 6B43, the 09.38 Eastleigh Yard to Southampton Western Docks trip working. Once again, a Class 67 on this train was probably due to the loco being in position at Eastleigh for a charter train, much of the stock for these trains being based at Eastleigh Depot at this time. 15 April 2011.

The ultimate in Class 67 freight haulage perhaps? This is the astonishing sight of 67005 *Queen's Messenger*, 67026 *Diamond Jubilee* and 67006 *Royal Sovereign* passing through Totton station with 6B93, the 09.38 Eastleigh to Fawley oil train. Not exactly the main reason for the repainting of these three Royal locos, but great to see nonetheless! 7 February 2013.

This is the return trip of that seen in the previous image, now with 67006 *Royal Sovereign*, 67026 *Diamond Jubilee* and 67005 *Queen's Messenger* passing through Redbridge with 6B94, the 12.00 Fawley to Eastleigh Yard. 7 February 2013.

Above: Not quite so outrageous as the last two images, but still rather impressive, this is 67006 *Royal Sovereign* and 67005 *Queen's Messenger* departing Eastleigh with a late running 6B43, the 09.38 Eastleigh Yard to Southampton Western Docks local trip working. 25 November 2011.

Left: The next two images show the first working of one of the class in the Salisbury area on freight. This is 67008 passing Salisbury station with 6Y26, the 09.08 Eastleigh Yard to Quidhampton empty china clay tanks. This long-standing service finally ceased running in 2009. 10 September 2003.

67008 is seen again with the return 6Y27, the 10.28 Quidhampton to Eastleigh, approaching Salisbury from the west. The Class 67s were recent arrivals in the Eastleigh area on driver training, as mentioned earlier, and this service was being used as another perfect opportunity. 10 September 2003.

It was perhaps inevitable that the class would eventually see use at some point on the annual railhead treatment trains (RHTT) that operate throughout the autumn across the UK. This is silver-liveried ex-Chiltern 67014 on the rear of 3J43, the 02.53 (Mondays-only) Didcot Yard to Didcot Yard working on the final part of this circuit passing Swindon. This service still operates at the time of writing but is now worked by DB Cargo Class 66s. 16 November 2015.

At this time, MoD workings to Ludgershall, near Andover, were in the hands of DB Schenker but have since been taken over by GBRf. 67022 and 67006 *Royal Sovereign* are seen at Andover coming off the main line and taking the branch with 6O19, the 08.18 Hinksey Yard to Ludgershall cable train. The train arrived here via the down main line from Basingstoke, seen to the top right of the picture to a point behind the photographer. It then shunted back over the points seen in the foreground to the up line. 6 September 2012.

As mentioned earlier, it is always amusing to see such small loads behind a locomotive, but even more so when this is behind a pair of Class 67s! This is the return working of the previous image, 6V39, the 12.02 Ludgershall to Didcot Yard, with just a single Warwell wagon in tow approaching Andover. The line through Ludgershall was originally a cross-country route that went through to Swindon but was closed in 1963. 6 September 2012.

Three years later, and the cable train is seen on the move once again. This is 67007 in the same spot as the previous image, again working as 6V39, the 12.02 Ludgershall to Didcot Yard. At the time of writing in 2021, this view is no longer possible because of the small conifer saplings seen in this image having burgeoned to about eight foot high or more! 12 March 2015.

This is not the first place you might associate with a Caledonian Sleeper-liveried Class 67. This is 67010 and 66110 passing Millbrook with 6B44, the 12.07 Southampton Western Docks to Eastleigh Yard trip working. The Class 67 was in the Eastleigh area for rectification at the depot and this train was being used as a test run for it. 19 February 2016.

This is 67012 hauling an unidentified Class 66 through Shawford with 6M44, the 12.30 Eastleigh Yard to Wembley, a train that no longer runs. 8 February 2008.

67021 is seen from Campbell Road Bridge approaching Eastleigh with 6B44, the 12.07 Southampton Western Docks to Eastleigh Yard trip working. This loco has since been painted in Pullman livery for use with the luxurious Belmond British Pullman train. 8 March 2011.

67025 *Western Star* is passing Southampton Central with 6B43, the 09.38 Eastleigh Yard to Southampton Western Docks trip working. 16 December 2011.

Above: As far as I can ascertain, this is the only time one of the fleet has worked this particular train. 67026 *Royal Diamond* is approaching Basingstoke with 6M48, the 10.34 Southampton Eastern Docks to Halewood (Jaguar) car train. It even worked the inbound train in the early hours that morning because of the non-availability of a Class 66. Often when that happens, there is a spare Class 66 in the Eastleigh area that can be used as a replacement. 15 June 2012.

Right: This must have been one of the shortest freight workings in the UK at the time. 67021 is approaching Eastleigh with the 6D83 Eastleigh Yard to Eastleigh T&RSMD conveying fuel tanks, all of about half a mile in distance! The train was not given a particular departure time, it basically departed when ready. 8 March 2011.

67025 *Western Star* is seen again working 6B44, the 12.07 Southampton Western Docks to Eastleigh Yard trip, this time passing through a rather damp St Denys station. 9 October 2012.

Chapter 3

Passenger Trains

The fleet has seen various use on timetabled passenger trains over the years, with an assortment of operators at one time or another, and still do in 2021. However, this is currently limited to only a couple of services for Transport for Wales (TfW).

In the mid-2000s, the class was used on a few summer-dated services for Virgin CrossCountry to help ease overcrowding problems on Voyagers heading to/from the popular West Country destinations. This is 67001 *Night Mail* with a nice uniform rake of ten Mk.2 air-cons forming 1V15, the 07.08 York to Paignton 'Holidaymaker' service, approaching Dawlish Warren. 14 August 2004.

This is 67005 *Queen's Messenger* departing Exeter St Davids' Platform 6 with 1M89, the 08.43 Paignton to Newcastle service. This was quite soon after the loco had been given the Royal livery. 14 August 2004.

Soon after the previous image, this is 67003 departing Exeter St Davids' Platform 5 with 1E99, the 09.05 Paignton-Newcastle service. This loco currently wears Arriva blue livery. 14 August 2004.

A small pool of the class is currently used on a couple of North to South Wales services with the loco operating in push-pull mode along with a Driving Van Trailer (DVT). This is 67022 propelling 1V91, the 05.33 Holyhead to Cardiff Central, crossing the River Usk on the approach to Newport. This was not actually one of the dedicated locos, but several of the fleet could substitute if required. 16 May 2016.

Seen from the same location at Newport, but this time looking in the opposite direction and with the loco leading, this is 67002, now in Arriva blue livery, coming off the line from Hereford and North Wales, again with 1V91, the 05.33 Holyhead to Cardiff Central service. 29 March 2012.

The same loco is once again up front a couple of years later as 67002 departs Newport with 1V91, the 05.33 Holyhead to Cardiff Central. The huge futuristic looking walkway above the lines is dominant in this image, but since electrification this view is now rather cluttered. 28 March 2014.

This time, the same loco is propelling as 67002 crosses the River Usk and approaches Newport with 1V91, the 05.33 Holyhead to Cardiff Central. 8 September 2014.

As mentioned earlier, various members of the class have appeared on these Arriva services, and this is ex-Chiltern silver-liveried 67014 arriving at Newport on time with 1V91 once again. 29 February 2016.

This is 67014 again, but this time propelling away from Manchester Piccadilly with 5D31, the 15.55 Manchester Piccadilly to Manchester Piccadilly via Longsight Depot empty stock. 23 September 2015.

This is the current situation at the time of writing. These trains are still Class 67 hauled/propelled but now use some redundant Mk.4 coaching stock and DVTs that were originally used on East Coast Main Line (ECML) trains before the advent of the new Class 800/801 units. This is colourful DVT 82216 arriving at Newport propelled by 67015 as 1V91, the 05.33 Holyhead to Cardiff Central. 23 November 2021.

This is 67015 departing Newport with 1W93, the 11.22 Cardiff Central to Holyhead, the return of the train seen in the previous image. Although there are a few Class 67s in Transport for Wales (TfW) livery, they are not always available for service. 23 November 2021.

Next, we have a series of images taken during the time when the class was being used on Bristol to Weymouth services during the late 2000s. Most of these trains were top and tailed, and this image shows 67003 on the rear of the recently arrived 2O72, the 09.09 from Bristol Temple Meads, pulling out of Weymouth station and heading for the sidings where it will then stable all day. 24 May 2008.

A couple of months later, and the same train was in the hands of 67025 *Western Star* and 67001. This is 67025 just coming to a halt at the Dorset seaside station. As always, any loco-hauled passenger trains are very popular with the enthusiast community these days. 26 July 2008.

This is 67001 (formerly *Night Mail*) on the other end of the train displaying a tail lamp. This is another loco currently in Arriva blue livery. 26 July 2008.

This service ran with Class 67s from 2007 to 2010 and, as far as I can tell, this is the only time just one loco was used, this being due to the non-availability of the second engine that morning. This is 67003 in a fine rural setting just south of Yeovil Pen Mill with 2O72, the 09.09 Bristol Temple Meads to Weymouth. The loco is now in Arriva blue livery. 5 June 2010.

67025 *Western Star* top and tails 67005 *Queen's Messenger* in the pouring rain at the sleepy wayside station at Maiden Newton with 2O72, the 09.09 Bristol Temple Meads to Weymouth. From here, the train will once again enter a single line section down to Dorchester West. 1 August 2009.

By that afternoon, the rain had cleared, and I was able to capture this view of 67005 *Queen's Messenger* with the return 2V67, the 16.50 Weymouth to Bristol Temple Meads, approaching Bincombe Tunnel, near the summit of the long climb out of the Dorset resort. Note the earthworks to the left that were the early stages of the Weymouth relief road construction, which opened to traffic in March 2011. 1 August 2009.

This is 67021 top and tailed with 67005 *Queen's Messenger* arriving at Dorchester West with 2O72, the 09.09 Bristol Temple Meads to Weymouth. At this time, severe tree cutting had recently taken place around here but, 14 years later, it had just about all grown up again! 14 July 2007.

During the last summer the Class 67s were used, it was perhaps inevitable that recently repainted 67018 *Keith Heller*, in a version of the new DB Schenker livery, would put in an appearance. Here, the loco is standing at Dorchester West, making an interesting comparison with the blue and grey coaches with 2V67, the 16.50 Weymouth to Bristol Temple Meads service. At the time of writing, this loco has been in storage for almost three years. 29 May 2010.

67017 *Arrow* leans into the curve at Stratton, just south of Maiden Newton, with 2V67, the 16.50 Weymouth to Bristol Temple Meads. This loco has since received TfW livery and normally works North to South Wales trains. It is hard to believe that the train is travelling over a line that was once a double-tracked main line throughout, seeing regular London Paddington to Weymouth expresses up until the 1960s. 23 May 2009.

Clattering along the old jointed bullhead track, 67006 *Royal Sovereign* leads 2O72, the 09.09 Bristol Temple Meads to Weymouth, at Queen Camel, between Castle Cary and Yeovil Pen Mill. 23 August 2008.

67017 *Arrow* is seen again, heading west with 2O72, the 09.09 Bristol Temple Meads to Weymouth, this time at Cole, just west of Bruton. This is the point where the Somerset and Dorset (S&D) line used to cross the Great Western line. Although the S&D line has been closed since 1966, the embankment here still stands defiantly. 27 June 2009.

DB red 67010 passes the same spot eight years later with 1O72, the 09.06 Bristol Temple Meads to Weymouth. This was the first non-railtour loco-hauled passenger train to Weymouth since 4 September 2010. It was operating in place of the booked HST, as that was required for additional services to Cardiff because of the Champions' League final taking place at the Millennium Stadium. The train consisted of considerably more coaches compared to the top and tailed services that operated previously. 3 June 2017.

We now move on to a few Wrexham & Shropshire/Chiltern Railways images. The small pool of six Class 67s worked these trains from 2010–14 when they were superseded by DRS Class 68s. You can almost feel the chill as 67012 *A Shropshire Lad* pulls away from the snowy Banbury stop with 1P03, the 07.23 Wrexham to London Marylebone, which was running very late due to the weather conditions. 7 January 2010.

A couple of years earlier, there was no such coldness on a fine spring morning. Complete with Wrexham & Shropshire branding, 67012 and 67014 are working top and tail as they approach Banbury with the 05.51 Wrexham to London Marylebone service. This was in the very early days of these services when they ran with a loco at each end and hired in coaching stock. The magnificent signal box and semaphores were all replaced in the mid-2010s, unfortunately. 2 May 2008.

This time we see 67015 *David J Lloyd* propelling the 08.20 London Marylebone to Kidderminster service. By this time, Wrexham & Shropshire had ceased to exist, and Chiltern Railways had taken over the running of these loco-hauled sets, now with dedicated Mk.3 stock and DVTs. 10 November 2011.

This is 67015 *David J Lloyd* again on the same day as the last image with the return 10.06 Kidderminster to London Marylebone passing Princes Risborough. The large disused signal box to the left of the picture was on the verge of being demolished around this time but, thankfully, it has been saved and is currently under restoration. 10 November 2011.

67008 is seen at Leamington Spa waiting to depart with 09.11 Marylebone to Birmingham Snow Hill. For some reason, this loco has a different typeface employed for the front end number. 24 September 2014.

Right: Passing the semaphore signals on the approach to Banbury, this is 67013 *Dyfrbont Pontcysyllte* with 1R22, the 10.15 London Marylebone to Birmingham Moor Street. As with the northern end of Banbury station, these semaphores and signal box have now vanished forever. The loco too has changed appearance, it now being de-named and wears DB Cargo red livery. 12 March 2013.

Below: This is 67017 *Arrow* arriving at Leamington Spa with an unidentified London Marylebone to Birmingham service. Note the wonderfully restored GWR station running in board, prominent to the left. 24 September 2014.

About 20 minutes later, at the same spot as the previous image, this is the now de-named 67013 arriving with another unidentified service from London Marylebone. 24 September 2014.

We now move on to a few images from the time the class was used on some South Wales to South West trains during the late 2000s and early 2010s. This image shows 67016 and 67017 *Arrow* passing Bristol Barton Hill depot with 2U14, the 11.02 Taunton to Cardiff Central. These trains always utilised the top and tail loco method rather than a DVT. 8 December 2009.

During 2010, the class was used further into the South West, this time extending from Taunton into Devon. 67018 *Keith Heller* top and tails with 67022 as it departs from Newton Abbot on the last few miles of its journey with 2C67, the 08.00 Cardiff Central to Paignton service. For many years, there was a large steam depot located in the area above the loco and train, which was later converted into a diesel depot in the mid-1960s, with many of the new Western Region diesel hydraulics being based there in their early days. 14 May 2010.

Keith Heller

67018 *Keith Heller* is seen again, this time at Bristol Temple Meads waiting to depart with 2U14, the 11.02 Taunton to Cardiff Central. This was during the period when two sets of loco-hauled stock using Class 67s, this set and one on the Taunton-Cardiff route, were in use in the area. 13 July 2010.

Right: Unfortunately, as of late 2021, this loco has been stored the longest of any of the class, since March 2015, and has been used as a source of spares for other locos. Only time will tell if it ever sees service again. In happier days, 67019 is seen passing what used to be the Malago Vale carriage sidings (to the left of image) on the outskirts of Bristol with 2U14, the 11.02 Taunton to Cardiff Central once again. 27 August 2010.

Below: 67028, however, has been more fortunate than its classmate and is currently still in traffic, wearing DB Cargo red livery. It is seen here on the rear of the train in the last image passing Malago Vale, Bristol. 27 August 2010.

Chapter 4
Charter Trains

One of the main duties for the fleet for quite some years now has been their use on various charter trains across the UK, a duty to which they are well suited.

The first part of this section depicts just a few of the general charters the class has worked. 67024 is captured soon after departure from Yeovil Junction on the Salisbury to Exeter line with 1Z82, the 08.02 London Waterloo to Axminster UK Railtours 'The Seaton Tramway 40th Anniversary Gala' charter. 67022 is bringing up the rear of the train. 6 June 2010.

This is 67022 later in the day (with 67024 now trailing) leading the return of the above charter. It has just exited Hewish Tunnel and is approaching Hewish Gates, just west of Crewkerne, with 1Z83, the 16.45 Axminster to London Waterloo. The class has never been common on this particular line, apart from the occasional appearance of the Colas Rail pair deputising for the New Measurement Train. 6 June 2010.

This is Royal-liveried 67006 *Royal Sovereign* at Berkeley Marsh, near Frome, with 1Z14, the 06.42 Letchworth to Paignton UK Railtours 'The Torbay Flyer'. 15 September 2018.

At the time, a Caledonian Sleeper-liveried member of the class was an unusual sight in the south, especially as they were not in this livery for very long. This, however, is 67010 (formerly *Unicorn*), which was in the area for maintenance at Eastleigh, approaching Basingstoke with 5O61, the 10.00 Wembley to Eastleigh empty stock. This was a semi-regular working when a charter had terminated in the London area the previous evening, the coaches then being tripped back to base at Eastleigh the next day. 13 June 2016.

This is 67016 approaching Mortimer on the Reading to Basingstoke line with an unidentified empty stock working to Eastleigh. 15 April 2010.

Rounding the long curve away from what used to be called Aller Junction, 67016 and 67024 are starting the climb up to Dainton with UK Railtours 'Mazey Day in Penzance' charter. With over 6,000hp available, there would be no problem tackling this stiff climb up to the summit at Dainton Tunnel. 26 June 2010.

67022 crosses Coombe Viaduct at Saltash with 1Z27, the 06.30 Lichfield Trent Valley to Par Past-Time Rail 'The Eden Flyer' heading for the Eden Project, which was a very popular destination for charter trains at that time. 12 June 2004.

67006 *Royal Sovereign* (with 67005 *Queen's Messenger* on the rear) is seen again, this time soon after departing Southampton Central with 1Z82, the 09.45 London Waterloo to Swanage Steam Dreams 'The Cathedrals Express'. On this occasion, the Class 67s were replacing steam loco 60163 *Tornado* because of the risk of lineside fires in the hot weather prevailing at the time. 9 July 2013.

Showing a few subtle livery differences, this is a nice pairing of DB red examples as 67015 and 67018 *Keith Heller* approach Eastleigh with 5O61, the 10.00 Wembley to Eastleigh. 14 December 2015.

Named pair 67025 *Western Star* and 67017 *Arrow* are seen approaching a nice tidy Swindon station (before the overhead electrification and associated clutter arrived!) with 1Z27, the 08.44 Huntingdon to Bristol Temple Meads charter. 3 December 2008.

Seen from the prominent location of Arnside Knot, Cumbria, this is 67028 crossing the Kent Estuary at Arnside with 1Z36, the 06.06 Cardiff Central to Carlisle 'The Cumbrian Coaster' organised by Pathfinder Tours. 27 July 2011.

Right: Back in the south of England, this is 67030 passing the classic location of the skew bridge at Teignmouth with the returning 1Z59, the 12.44 Bodmin Parkway to Trowbridge. This was a private charter provided for the staff of a factory located at the White Horse Business Park in Trowbridge. 11 February 2011.

Below: With some lovely autumn colours to the trees, silver pair 67029 *Royal Diamond* and 67014 make another interesting comparison in liveries as they approach Basingstoke with 5O61, the 10.00 Wembley to Eastleigh empty stock. 31 October 2016.

This is 67030 again, this time approaching Lambert's Bridge soon after departing Westbury with 1Z27, the 06.15 Reading to Kingswear Pathfinder Tours 'The Torbay & Dartmouth Explorer'. This loco has currently been in storage since 2019. 30 September 2017.

This is 67027 *Rising Star* on the rear of the 07.38 Hove to Par Past-Time Rail 'The Eden Flyer' charter as it passes through Salisbury station. 15 July 2006.

As mentioned earlier, the Eden Project was a very popular destination in its early days, with charters coming from virtually all over the country. Here is another one, this time headed by 67026, passing through Dawlish Warren with 1Z80, the 06.00 Tonbridge to Par Past-Time Rail 'The Eden Flyer'. 14 August 2004.

Right: This is 67030 and 67026 arriving at Westbury with 1Z28, the 06.11 Cambridge to Minehead UK Railtours 'The West Somerset Railway Spring Steam Gala' charter, heading for another of the southwest's fine attractions. 28 March 2009.

Below: The Royal pair are often used on charters when not required for Royal duties. This is 67006 *Royal Sovereign* departing Dorchester South with 1Z92, the 07.09 Peterborough to Weymouth 'Dorset Maiden' charter. Until recently, this cutting was covered in large trees totally masking this view. 24 July 2021.

On the other end of the train was 67005 *Queen's Messenger* and it is seen passing Dorchester South with the 5Z93 empty stock from Weymouth. Normally, the empties would stable in the sidings at Weymouth all day but at this time they were closed for planned maintenance, thus meaning the train had to come back up and stable in the down platform at Dorchester South. 24 July 2021.

This is 67029 *Royal Diamond* approaching Worgret Junction on the single line from Swanage with 1Z83, the 17.05 Swanage to London Waterloo, which was the return of UK Railtours 'The Purbeck Tornado' charter. Steam loco 60163 *Tornado* had brought the train down from London and was on the rear at this point as far as Southampton Up Loop, it would then lead back to London via Andover and Basingstoke. At the time, this particular location was still under Network Rail jurisdiction but has since passed over to the Swanage Railway. 16 June 2010.

Another colourful pairing of 67014 and 67018 *Keith Heller* is seen speeding south past the Baltic Siding on the approach to Winchester with 5O61, the 10.00 Wembley to Eastleigh. 29 August 2016.

Very soon after the formation of Wrexham & Shropshire, there was rather a surprising sight at Poole station of two recently ex works silver-liveried members of the class on a charter! 67014 is seen departing the sidings to form 1Z58, the 16.00 Poole to Hooton charter. This was organised by Chester Model Railway Club/Ffestiniog Railway (Dee & Mersey Group) and entitled 'The Dorset Coast Express'. Unfortunately for the punters and photographers alike, it was a very wet day, but the sight of freshly painted silver locos and ex-Virgin stock a long way from their sphere of operations was not to be missed. 19 April 2008.

This is 67015 on the rear of the above charter just pulling away from a thoroughly wet Poole station. 19 April 2008.

The first of another four views of 5O61, the 10.00 Wembley Yard to Eastleigh charter empty stock. 67019 (stored since March 2015) is seen approaching Eastleigh. An unidentified member of the class is on the rear. 22 July 2011.

Four years later, and the empty stock is seen approaching Basingstoke in the hands of silver-liveried 67014. 6 July 2015.

With extra embellishments on the bodyside proclaiming 'First Choice for Rail Freight in the UK', this is DB-liveried 67013 about to pass through Basingstoke station. 3 September 2018.

This time we see 67022 just east of Farnborough heading south with the train. Recent lineside clearance at the time had opened up this previously lost location, but needless to say that in just five years or so this has all but grown up again! 6 June 2016.

This is 67005 *Queen's Messenger* approaching Parson Street, on the outskirts of Bristol, with 1Z97, the 08.15 Eastleigh to Kingswear Pathfinder Tours 'The Torbay Flyer' charter. 27 August 2010.

Three of the class were repainted in Arriva Trains' blue livery in the mid-2010s and this is 67003 at Bristol Temple Meads with 1Z23, the 06.50 Cambridge to Taunton UK Railtours 'Somerset, Jewel of the South West' charter. Passengers on this trip were given the options of either a road coach to visit the Dean Forest Railway from Bristol or to Hestercombe House and gardens by road coach from Taunton. 4 July 2015.

Just prior to becoming a Royal loco, 67006 is seen at Berkeley Marsh, near Frome, with 1C52, the 07.25 London Paddington to Paignton Hertfordshire Rail Tours charter. 22 May 2004.

For the next part of this section on charters, I have included a few images of the Royal Train, which can just about be classed as a charter! Having dropped the Royal contingent in Weymouth, this is 67005 *Queen's Messenger* leading (with 67006 *Royal Sovereign* on the rear) with the returning stock at Bincombe, between Weymouth and Dorchester, heading for its base at Wolverton. 11 June 2009.

A few years later, and we see 67005 *Queen's Messenger* top and tailing 67006 *Royal Sovereign* on a slightly shorter formation passing Basingstoke and taking the line towards Reading. 9 June 2017.

It has not always been 67005 and 67006 that have worked the Royal Train. 67026 received a silver livery, a large Union flag and a special logo for use during the Diamond Jubilee celebrations in 2012. It was named *Diamond Jubilee* by Her Majesty on 23 March 2012 at London Victoria station. The immaculate loco is seen arriving at Salisbury station with HM The Queen on board as part of the countrywide tour that year. 1 May 2012.

A further view of 67026 *Diamond Jubilee* as it departs from Salisbury with the empty stock. Despite all this pomp and ceremony, this is, unfortunately, another member of the fleet in storage (since 2016), and it is unknown when or if the loco will return to service. 1 May 2012.

Another reserve loco for the Royal Train has been 67029 *Royal Diamond*. It was named on 12 October 2007 at Rugeley Trent Valley station in honour of the 60th wedding anniversary of HM Queen Elizabeth II and Prince Philip. It is seen just a month later passing Reading with an unknown working bound for London; note the addition of a pair of flags on the front of the loco. This loco was stored in May 2020. 7 November 2007.

Both the dedicated locos received a slightly revised Royal livery during 2018. This is 67005 *Queen's Messenger* looking absolutely spotless as it passes Berkeley Marsh, near Frome, with a Castle Cary to London empty stock working. 67006 *Royal Sovereign* was bringing up the rear. 28 March 2019.

The bulk of this section on charters focuses on another of the prestigious workings that has been entrusted to the class for many years now, the famous Belmond British Pullman train (formerly the VSOE) that regularly runs throughout the year, mainly in the south of England. This is 67023 passing St Denys with 1Z93, the 13.10 Basingstoke to Bournemouth via Andover luncheon from Bournemouth. 9 September 2010.

67021 is seen two years earlier at Lymington Junction, just south of Brockenhurst, and running to the same itinerary as seen in the previous image, but this time heading in the opposite direction from Bournemouth to Basingstoke. 26 September 2008.

This is 67024 passing Wimbledon West Junction and heading west with one of the regular Pullman lunch services that run via a circular route from London Victoria. 4 July 2014.

This is 67019 (with 67016 out of sight on the rear) passing Southampton Central with 1Z89, the 13.13 Basingstoke to Bournemouth Pullman dining charter. 22 October 2010.

A year later, and Arriva blue-liveried 67003 (with 67030 out of sight on the rear) is passing the same spot at Southampton Central, but this time on a circular routing with 1Z91, the 10.40 Winchester to Southampton Airport Parkway that was routed via Romsey, Westbury, Melksham and Basingstoke. 14 October 2011.

This is silver 67015 approaching Basingstoke with semi-regular 1V80, the 09.49 London Victoria to Bath Spa. This one is also sometimes steam hauled on various dates during the year. 23 October 2013.

From above the twin tunnels at Popham (near Micheldever), we see 67008 and 67001 heading north with 1Z92, the 11.38 Bournemouth to Basingstoke dining train. 2 October 2009.

Looking smart in DB red livery, 67015 passes Clapham Junction Platform 5 with a special 10.00 London Victoria to Worcester Shrub Hill charter. 9 July 2016.

Back to the Bournemouth main line, and 67002 *Special Delivery* and 67001 (formerly *Night Mail*) are seen heading down the long Christchurch Bank with the 5Z89 Stewarts Lane to Bournemouth empty stock for the working seen in the next image. 3 October 2008.

After loading the customers at Bournemouth, this is 67001 passing Christchurch with 1Z92, the 11.38 Bournemouth to Bournemouth via Basingstoke dining train. 3 October 2008.

Left: With both locos visible on the tight curve, 67015 and 67018 *Keith Heller* are passing Eastleigh with 5Z88, the 12.00 Chichester to Eastleigh T&RSMD. The train had run that morning from London Victoria to Chichester and was heading to Eastleigh Depot (via the East Yard) for servicing and a return later in the day. 29 July 2016.

Below: Of all the 30 locos of the class, 67004 always seems to be quite rare in the south. It is seen here, however, at London Victoria with the 1Z13, the 10.15 London Victoria to Winchester charter. This loco was stored in May 2020. 30 November 2018.

Seen from the large footbridge that crosses the station at Clapham Junction, this is another view of 67004 with the train seen in the last image negotiating the pointwork to pass Platform 6. 30 November 2018.

During 2017, 67021 and 67024 were painted in Pullman livery to match the stock. This is 67021 stood at Salisbury with 1V80, the 09.43 London Victoria to Bath Spa. This was one of its first trips in this livery and was yet to receive any branding. 6 December 2017.

This is the equally immaculate 67024 on the other end of the train in the previous image, also at Salisbury. 6 December 2017.

On a lovely autumn afternoon, 67003 with 67030 on the rear passes Mount Pleasant, just south of St Denys, with 5Z92, the 14.56 Southampton Airport Parkway to Eastleigh via a reversal in Southampton Down Loop. Unfortunately, both of these locos were stored in October 2019. 14 October 2011.

On a gloomy day, this is 67006 *Royal Sovereign* exiting the British Pullman's home depot of Stewarts Lane with empty stock bound for London Victoria for a Remembrance Day special working. On this particular day, it pulled up beside Wandsworth Road station (from where this image was taken) and the loco on the other end of the train, 67014, then proceeded in to London Victoria station on the lines to the right of this image. 11 November 2011.

67024 is this time approaching Salisbury with the Newbury to Salisbury East Yard empty stock from a special London Victoria to Newbury charter that operated earlier in the day. Although the Pullmans are common at Salisbury, it is rare to see them in the early afternoon arriving from the western direction. 29 September 2021.

The classic location of Campbell Road Bridge at Eastleigh sees 67001 departing with 5Z92, the 07.10 Stewarts Lane to Bournemouth empty stock, with 67008 on the back. 2 October 2009

Right: Although the dedicated 67021 and 67024 are always used when possible, there are times when one or both are out of service for one reason or another and other locos substitute. 67028 is seen at Upton Scudamore with 1Z83, the 11.00 Chichester to Westbury via Netley and Southampton luncheon charter. 16 August 2013.

Below: This is the same train as the previous image, now with 67006 *Royal Sovereign* leading on the return, just about to top the climb from Westbury at Upton Scudamore with 1Z84, the 13.44 Westbury to Chichester via Chandlers Ford and Eastleigh. This was part of a day-long excursion. 16 August 2013.

67006
Royal Sovereign

Above: Recent trackside clearance had opened up this shot in the heart of the New Forest at Woodfiddley, between Beaulieu Road and Brockenhurst, providing a nice clear shot of 67029 *Royal Diamond* and 67006 *Royal Sovereign* with 1Z92, the 11.38 Bournemouth to Basingstoke. Needless to say, that in the intervening years since this was taken, it has all long since grown back again! 16 April 2010.

Left: DB red 67018 *Keith Heller* makes a colourful sight as it heads past Millbrook Freightliner Terminal with 1Z93, the 13.12 Basingstoke to Bournemouth. This loco was stored in March 2019. 25 May 2011.

These days it is rare to see any sort of loco-hauled train at the busy location of Surbiton, but this is 67006 *Royal Sovereign* passing through with 1V80, the 09.49 London Victoria to Bath Spa. These charters are more often routed via Staines to re-join the South Western Main Line at Byfleet & New Haw, thus avoiding the Surbiton area during the busiest times. 10 December 2008.

Above: Another rare loco in the south is 67030 (with 67003 on the rear) seen here at Worting Junction, just west of Basingstoke, with 5Z92, the 07.00 Stewarts Lane to Bournemouth. 21 October 2011.

Right: 67002 *Special Delivery* is passing Lymington Junction with the 5Z89 Stewarts Lane to Bournemouth empty stock. The line to the right of the picture is the branch to Lymington. 26 September 2008.

During the early days of Class 67 haulage on the Pullmans, this is 67010 *Unicorn* at Westbury with an unidentified service waiting to head west. This loco is now in DB Cargo's bright red livery. 12 September 2003.

Seen from Alexandra Park Gardens, high above the magnificent city of Bath, this is 67022 arriving with 1V80, the 09.44 London Victoria to Bath Spa. This was a very cold day, and a sprinkling of snow is evident. This loco was stored in June 2019. 1 December 2010.

Not very far from the location seen in the previous image, this is another fine spot, with the River Avon prominent in the foreground. This is 67005 *Queen's Messenger* soon after passing through Avoncliffe Halt, situated in the picturesque Avon Valley with 1Z76, the 09.15 London Victoria to Bath Spa. 18 April 2015.

67018 *Keith Heller* is seen again, approaching Hawkeridge Junction near Westbury. This was a private charter using the Pullmans, the 1Z16 Bristol Temple Meads to London Victoria. 21 November 2015.

It is not every day you see the Pullmans here, at least not for over 50 years! This is 67006 *Royal Sovereign* shunting the empty stock at Bournemouth West Depot for servicing, the train having arrived at Bournemouth earlier in the morning from London. This was believed to be the first time any Pullman stock had been seen here since 1967 when the famous Bournemouth Belle train last ran. In fact, two coaches, *Zena* and *Ione*, were once part of that very train. The point on which the train is standing used to be a pair of main running lines that lead to the terminus station at Bournemouth West until the late 1960s when the depot and sidings were completely remodelled, and West station closed. 1 September 2007.

This time we see 67009 powering towards St Denys, just north of Southampton Central, with 1Z92, the 11.38 Bournemouth to Basingstoke. This loco was stored back in October 2016. 9 September 2010.

The road bridge at Westbury has always been a good place to watch proceedings in and around the station. This is 67021 departing from the station with 1V80, the 09.49 London Victoria to Bath Spa. 12 February 2020.

Looking the other way on the same bridge, we see 67024 bringing up the rear of 1V80 as it curves away on to the Trowbridge line towards Bath. 12 February 2020.

Only occasionally are the Pullmans double headed; this is Royal pair 67006 *Royal Sovereign* and 67005 *Queen's Messenger* powering through Taunton with 1Z78, the 09.48 London Victoria to Truro, which was the start of a weekend tour of the West Country, which has become an annual event since this date. 14 May 2010.

It can only be springtime in the Wylye Valley as 67006 *Royal Sovereign* and 67029 *Royal Diamond* bisect the bright yellow rapeseed fields at Wylye level crossing with 1V80, the 09.43 London Victoria to Bath. 26 April 2017.

67006 *Royal Sovereign* is seen again, this time in the heart of the New Forest National Park at the start of the long curve at Woodfiddley, between Beaulieu Road and Brockenhurst, with 5Z92, the 07.10 Stewarts Lane to Bournemouth. Once again, this spot has now long since grown over with trees and bushes. 16 April 2010.

This time we are in the South London suburbs at Putney as 67021 approaches with a special 1Z40, the 10.46 London Victoria to Portsmouth Harbour. 21 September 2018.

Coming round the curve between the Southampton Maritime and Millbrook Freightliner terminals, 67022 heads north with 1Z92, the 11.37 Bournemouth to Basingstoke. The footbridge from which this view was taken has since closed, as it was deemed to be dangerous. 25 May 2011.

To conclude this section, we are still in South London, this time with 67024 on the rear of 1Z52, the 08.31 London Victoria to Watlington special service passing Kensington Olympia. 10 October 2018.

Chapter 5
Test Trains

Class 67s began to be used on various test trains up and down the UK upon EWS' withdrawal of its last few remaining Class 47s and 37s in the early 2000s. However, these were also later displaced by DRS traction and, later still, Colas Rail. The latter went on to purchase two Class 67s from DB Cargo in the mid-2010s, mainly to substitute for the New Measurement Train (NMT).

Before its later makeover as a Royal loco, 67006 is seen entering Poole station from the south with an unidentified test train that had visited the Hamworthy branch line and Weymouth. 29 March 2004.

Above: This is 67023 and 67008 passing Sprey Point near Teignmouth with 1Q19, the 11.05 Plymouth to London Paddington NMT replacement. Ever since the introduction of the NMT in 2003, there have been times when it was out of service, thus Class 67s have regularly substituted for it. 31 July 2015.

Left: In top and tail format, 67021 and 67028 are seen approaching a public foot crossing just west of Salisbury with a track recording train heading eastbound towards Salisbury station. 18 January 2006.

Over the years, test train circuits have changed quite a lot. This is 67020 and 67021 arriving at Brockenhurst with a morning service that originated at Eastleigh, a train that has long since ceased to run. 9 July 2004.

This is 67021 on the eastern end of the train in the last view now waiting to depart eastbound back towards Southampton. It was one of the few loco-hauled trains that used this up loop platform at Brockenhurst. 9 July 2004.

In the days before it was repainted silver for Wrexham & Shropshire, 67014 stands in the sunshine at Weymouth station with a 1Q14 service that had originated at Eastleigh and covered a few former Southern Region lines before heading back to Eastleigh. 4 October 2004.

Making a welcome change from the usual Class 158/159 units on the Salisbury to Exeter line, this is 67020 passing the seldom photographed Tisbury station with 1Q23, the 04.45 Old Oak Common to Salisbury via Exeter NMT replacement. 18 September 2014.

On the rear of the train in the last image was 67030, making a rare appearance in the south. At the time it was fitted with Radio Electronic Token Block (RETB) for use in Scotland. This image was taken from what was originally the old down platform that was taken out of service when the line was singled back in the late 1960s. 18 September 2014.

When 1Q23 arrived back at Salisbury, the train changed its reporting number and made a trip to Southampton and back running as 1X23, the 13.10 Salisbury to Old Oak Common. This is a view of 67030 arriving at Southampton Central. 18 September 2014.

This is 67020 arriving back at Salisbury after its run to Southampton and back with 1X23, the 13.10 Salisbury to Old Oak Common NMT replacement. 18 September 2014.

The last picture from this day shows 67030 preparing to depart Salisbury with 1X23, the 13.10 Salisbury to Old Oak Common on its last leg back to London. 18 September 2014.

This time we see 67006 *Royal Sovereign* and a hidden 67026 *Diamond Jubilee* with 1Q23, the 04.51 Old Oak Common to Salisbury via Exeter and Yeovil NMT replacement, passing the remains of the long-closed station of Semley (between Tisbury and Gillingham) on the Salisbury to Exeter line. This was once the station that served the North Dorset town of Shaftesbury, around three miles away. Surprisingly, the station infrastructure here is still pretty intact despite having closed back in 1966, with the goods shed, station buildings and even the old signal box still in situ, but in varying states of repair. It is always quite an event when any loco-hauled train appears on this line nowadays. 20 December 2012.

South Wales this time and the Usk Bridge at Newport as 67027 heads (with 67020 bringing up the rear) 1Z20, the 05.37 Old Oak Common to Derby RTC. This loco was only in DB red for about a year, so images in this livery are not that common. 28 March 2014.

This is a colourful eye-catching ensemble with 67027 and 67014 taking the Didcot Parkway avoiding line with 1Q05, the 11.00 Old Oak Common to Derby RTC. 2 January 2015.

An almost impossible to imagine combination, seen here on the Great Western Main Line at Swindon of all places! Despite a thoroughly miserable day, it was important to record this working as it was the first visit of an electric loco in the daylight here, albeit not powering solo. This is 5Q91, the 09.19 Swindon Transfer Sidings to Didcot Parkway formed of 67028, Data and Acquisition Test Services (DATS)-owned Mk.3s 82115 and 11074, DB Cargo's 90035 (fitted with a modified recording, non-power collection pantograph) and 67012 on the rear. The ensemble is arriving from the sidings into Swindon station to prepare for the first of a couple of runs to Didcot and back. 15 November 2019.

The first of three images of another unusual combination, this is former Chiltern Railways 67012 *A Shropshire Lad* passing the turntable and a nice crop of tulips as it departs Yeovil Junction with 1Q23, the 04.48 Old Oak Common to Salisbury via Exeter test train. The reason for the short-formed train utilising just one loco was due to the failure of another Class 67 earlier that morning; rather surprisingly, it was not cancelled altogether. 16 April 2015.

With the loco having run-round at Exeter St Davids, this is a view of the same train departing Exeter Central on its way back to Salisbury. This was once a very busy station in its heyday but is now much reduced in importance with only a couple of tracks now in use. There was also a large signal box to the right of the loco that has long since vanished. 16 April 2015.

Further east up the line, spring is most definitely in the air here at Gillingham as 67012 with 1Q23 awaits a London Waterloo to Exeter St Davids train to come off the single line ahead before departure for Salisbury. 16 April 2015.

Since 2015, most Network Rail test trains in the UK have been operated using Colas Rail traction. To conclude this section on test trains, we see dedicated Colas pair 67023 and 67027, which were sold by DB Cargo in early 2017, in action at various locations in the south of England. On one of the pair's first trips since being painted in Colas house colours, this is 67023 stood at Newbury Racecourse station on a day of sunshine and showers with 1Z78, the 06.05 Tyseley to Bristol High Level Siding, which is another working that seems to have vanished in more recent years. 22 March 2017.

There was a layover of around 45 minutes for the train here at Newbury Racecourse. Ready to lead the train back in the direction it arrived from, this is 67027 ticking over patiently in the platform. 22 March 2017.

Both locos were named during June 2017, and in the case of 67027, it was its second name. This is 67023 *Stella* approaching Westbury with 67027 *Charlotte* bringing up the rear of 1Z22, the 08.14 Tyseley to Bristol High Level Siding via Weymouth service. 5 September 2018.

The first of two images taken at Yeovil Pen Mill, which is a rare location in the south still clinging on to its semaphore signals. 67027 *Charlotte* approaches with 1Z22, the 08.14 Tyseley to Bristol High Level Siding. There is also a signal box still in use here, just out of sight to the left of the picture. 4 October 2017.

Right: It is always interesting to see a combination of old railway infrastructure alongside more modern designs. This is 67023 *Stella* on the rear of 1Z22 as it heads away south from Yeovil Pen Mill to Dorchester and Weymouth past the fine semaphore display. 4 October 2017.

Below: Both locos are seen to good advantage as 67023 leads (to the left) with 67027 on the rear, both prior to being named. The train is once again 1Z22, the 08.14 Tyseley to Bristol High Level Siding, this time in the heart of the fine Somerset countryside on the approach to Castle Cary. 19 April 2017.

Charlotte

67027 *Charlotte* arrives at Didcot Parkway with 1Z23, the 07.13 Bristol High Level Siding to Tyseley The train will reverse here and take the northbound route via Oxford and Leamington Spa. 9 August 2018.

Further southwest again now as we see 67023 *Stella* leading 1Q23, the 05.46 Reading Triangle Sidings to Salisbury, passing through Exeter Central. The wide gap between the running lines signifies that there were once two more centre lines, and in the background, the huge apartment block is built on the site of the old freight distribution point. 29 June 2017.

Stella

Later the same day, the train arrives at Gillingham where a stop was made to cross a London Waterloo to Exeter St Davids service train. The signal box to the left of the picture closed with the re-signalling of the line in 2012 but is retained for use by the engineering department as a ground frame. 29 June 2017.

Slowly passing Exeter St Davids, 67027 *Charlotte* is seen leading 1Q23, the 05.41 Reading Triangle Sidings to Salisbury via Exeter New Yard. There is usually an hour's layover in the yard at Exeter before making its return run. 17 December 2020.

This is 67023 *Stella* passing through the same platform at Exeter St Davids with the commencement of 1Q23 seen in the previous shot. 17 December 2020.

A minor dilemma is occurring here at Salisbury station. One of the windscreen wipers on 67023 *Stella* has become faulty, but, fortunately, it was soon rectified by the driver and a couple of the staff on board 1Q23, the 04.56 Old Oak Common to Salisbury, so the train could safely continue on its journey. 14 December 2017.

On a lovely fresh early summer morning we see 67027 *Charlotte* on the rear of the 1Q23 05.41 Reading Triangle Sidings to Salisbury passing near the village of Motcombe, situated just a couple of miles east of Gillingham, on the edge of the delightful Blackmore Vale. 28 June 2018.

On the western side of Gillingham lies the well-known location of Buckhorn Weston Tunnel, where we see 67023 *Stella* in the bright summer sunshine heading east with 1Q23, the 05.41 Reading Triangle Sidings to Salisbury. Again, this was once a double track main line at this point. 4 July 2019.

67023 *Stella* is seen again, bringing up the rear of the same train as the previous image, but three months later and passing the former station at Semley on the Wiltshire/Dorset border. 24 October 2019.

Seen from the platform now used by the South West Mainline Steam Co, the viewer is left in no doubt where 67027 *Charlotte* is seen with 1Q23, the 04.56 Old Oak Common to Salisbury. 29 June 2017.

The final image in this section was taken later on the same morning as the previous picture. This is 67027 *Charlotte* disappearing beneath New Road Bridge at Exeter Central, now on the rear of 1Q23 as it heads eastwards back to Salisbury. 29 June 2017.

Chapter 6
Miscellaneous Views

The last section of this book depicts a few images that do not really fit in any of the previous categories or are at unusual locations.

In the early days, a good place to see one or two of the class was often Plymouth station, where they could be found stabled for use on mail trains. This is 67007, recognisable at the time by having no running number on one cab front, coupled to 67023 in the middle road, having just arrived light engines from St Blazey depot. 1 August 2002.

Another good spot to find one or two of the fleet lurking was in the bay platforms at the western end of Plymouth station. This is 67004 *Post Haste* and 67015 awaiting their next duties. 14 March 2002.

Class 67s have occasionally been used on unit drags down the years; these next images show just a few of these. This is 67005 *Queen's Messenger* approaching Shawford as it heads north with 5X70, the 14.00 Eastleigh Yard to Bescot hauling Class 508s 508302 and 508303. 18 November 2009.

67008 is seen at Eastleigh heading into the works complex with a pair of barrier coaches that were being used in conjunction with moving Class 395 Javelin units for South Eastern, these being delivered to Southampton Docks around this time. 14 January 2005.

During the mid-2000s, the Class 377 Electrostars were slowly being introduced into service, but they suffered quite a few setbacks during the process. This resulted in a few of the class briefly being stored at MoD Marchwood in Hampshire of all places until they were ready to enter traffic. With an unusually large amount of clag being emitted for a Class 67, this is 67017 *Arrow* departing Eastleigh with a pair of barrier coaches en route to Marchwood to collect a unit. 24 January 2005.

Later in the day, 67017 *Arrow* is seen hauling an unidentified Class 377 from Freemantle footbridge on the approach to Southampton Central. 24 January 2005.

After running round in the sidings at Poole, this is 67019 coming up the 1 in 60 gradient of Parkstone Bank hauling two withdrawn slam door units. Most of these moves saw the units head for Caerwent, South Wales, for breaking up, but I believe these two were off to the Dean Forest Railway for preservation and were the last two to leave Bournemouth Depot. 5 July 2005.

Since their early days, various members of the fleet have acted as thunderbirds at various points along the length of the ECML to recover any failures that may occur to the Class 91 locos that worked the line regularly until recently. These Class 91 workings have been drastically reduced with the introduction of the Class 800–803 units that entered service in the late 2010s and early 2020s, although a few diagrams still remain at the time of writing. This is 67013 parked in the bay at Newcastle awaiting the call. 30 December 2003.

With its additional 'First Choice for Rail Freight in the UK' branding emblazoned on the bodyside, 67010 is seen in the usual thunderbird stabling spot under the footbridge at Doncaster, beside the station. 12 February 2019.

A sparkling ex works TfW-liveried 67025 is seen stabled at Eastleigh. Although this loco had literally just been repainted, it was not done at the nearby works. It was in the area for testing with modified Mk.4 coaching stock that TfW had recently acquired at the time. 11 November 2019.

Yes, it is certainly not a Class 67, but I felt I had to include this unusual working! The bizarre ensemble of 46035, 67024, 5051 *Earl Bathurst* and 67025 *Western Star* on the rear of 5A24, the 07.45 Bristol Barton Hill to Old Oak Common, is seen just after arrival at Didcot Parkway. This was a service that ran on Wednesdays-only to trip postal vans for maintenance at the London depot but, on this day, it was also used to move the Class 46 and steam loco to Didcot after being involved in a charter the previous weekend in the Bristol area, thus avoiding a separate movement. The Class 46 and Castle loco are no longer main line registered at the time of writing in late 2021. 14 May 2003.

Another unusual place to see one of the class is in Didcot Yard. This is 67020, which is believed to have arrived with a MoD container service from Marchwood Military Port. 20 January 2014.

This is another of those untimed moves that start from Eastleigh East Yard and travel the short distance to the works that we saw earlier. This is 67018 *Keith Heller* with the 6D83 Eastleigh Yard to Eastleigh T&RSMD hauling Mk.2f coaches 3400 and 9522 along with three TTA tank wagons, probably all heading for maintenance in the works. 31 March 2011.

This time we see 67028 with 'Leading The Next Generation of Rail Freight' on the bodyside arriving at Salisbury hauling recently overhauled Hanson & Hall-owed 50008 *Thunderer* as 0Z50, the 13.32 Eastleigh Works to Salisbury. This was the first of a few test runs for the Class 50 with the 67 being brought along just in case. 7 June 2021.

Not exactly an unusual working but sometimes going to some unusual places, this is the DB management train. To date, this is the first and only time it has traversed the Yeovil to Weymouth line and is seen passing the tiny station at Chetnole, just north of Maiden Newton, with semi-dedicated 67029 *Royal Diamond* propelling 1Z06, the 10.10 Weymouth to Llandindrod Wells. 12 May 2010.

Again, we see 67029 *Royal Diamond* propelling, this time on 1Z05, the 10.42 Southampton Central to London Gateway, arriving to pick up its guests at Southampton Central station. 3 June 2016.

And yet again propelling, 67029 *Royal Diamond* departs Torquay with the empty stock as 5Z05, the 12.34 Torquay to Goodrington Sidings (Paignton). The train had arrived at Torquay about five minutes earlier as 1Z05, the 08.31 Ealing Broadway to Torquay. It stabled overnight at Goodrington before returning north the following day. 23 April 2015.

With 67029 currently stored, other Class 67s have been recorded on the DB management train at times. On one such occasion, 67015 has just departed Bath Spa with 1Z06, the 13.18 Westbury to Toton, and is approaching Oldfield Park station. 14 October 2019.

The last few images in this section, and indeed this volume, focus on a few of the class that have so far paid a visit to the Swanage Railway in Dorset. This is the first of four images that show the first ever visit of a member of the class when 67026 worked 0Z50, the 08.14 Eastleigh Yard to Swanage, to collect ballast wagons that had been in use on the heritage line for a few weeks. It is seen here at Corfe Castle waiting to depart with 6Z50, the 12.51 Swanage to Eastleigh Yard return, although actually starting from Corfe Castle. 2 February 2010.

Above: By the time the train was on the move, there was a hint of light snow in the air on this cold day as we see 6Z50 crossing Corfe Castle Viaduct with its long rake of hoppers. 2 February 2010.

Right: We now see 6Z50 on what was back then still Network Rail metals at Furzebrook with about two miles to go to reach the main line. This section of line was upgraded a few years after this view and now comes under Swanage Railway jurisdiction. 2 February 2010.

The last shot of this train sees it arriving back out on the main line as it passes Worgret Junction and makes its way towards Wareham station, initially for about a mile travelling over the down line but crossing to the up line just before the station is reached. 2 February 2010.

Although these last two images are of charters, I have included them in this section due to being photographed on the heritage line, not the national network. The delightful surroundings of the Purbeck Hills are the backdrop here as 67029 *Royal Diamond* slowly heads away from Swanage and passes over the crossing at Quarr Farm, just south of Harmans Cross, with 1Z83, the 17.05 Swanage to London Waterloo 'Purbeck Tornado'. Steam loco 60163 was out of sight on the rear at this point. 16 June 2010.

This time 67028 is seen passing the Harmans Cross down starting signal with 1Z98, the 17.10 Swanage to London Waterloo UK Railtours 'The Royal Wessex'. This time Merchant Navy 35028 *Clan Line* was out of sight on the rear. 27 April 2012.